The Medieval World

Kathy Elgin

Produced for Chelsea House by Bailey Publishing Associates Ltd, 11a Woodlands, Hove BN3 6TJ, England

Library of Congress Cataloging-in-Publication Data
Elgin, Kathy.
  The medieval world / Kathy Elgin.
    p. cm. — (Costume source books)
  Includes bibliographical references and index.
  ISBN 978-1-60413-378-3
  1. Clothing and dress—History—Medieval, 500-1500—Juvenile literature. I. Title. II. Series.

GT575.E54 2009
391.00902—dc22

2008047259

Project Manager: Patience Coster
Text design by Jane Hawkins
Picture Research: Shelley Noronha
Artists: Deirdre Clancy Steer (pages 17, 25, 47, 56); Sam Steer (page 35)
Cover printed by Creative Printing, Hong Kong
Book printed and bound by Creative Printing, Hong Kong
Date printed: February, 2010
Printed in China

10 9 8 7 6 5 4 3 2

The publishers would like to thank the following for permission to reproduce their pictures: Bailey Publishing Associates Ltd: 7, 19; Bridgeman Art Library: 6 (British Library, London, UK/© British Library Board. All rights reserved.), 6 *detail* and 10 (Art Gallery of New South Wales, Sydney, Australia), 11 (Bibliothèque de l'Arsenal, Paris, France/Archives Charmet), *title page detail* and 12 *detail* (Musée National du Moyen Âge et des Thermes de Cluny, Paris/Lauros/Giraudon), 14 (Private Collection/Ken Welsh), 16 (Musée Condé, Chantilly, France/Index), 20 (Private Collection/© The Fine Art Society, London, UK), 22 *detail* (Burrell Collection, Glasgow, Scotland/© Glasgow City Council, Museums), 26 (Palazzo Ducale, Mantua, Italy), 32 (Musée de la Tapisserie, Bayeux, France/with special authorization of the city of Bayeux), 34 (Gemäldegalerie Alte Meister, Kassel, Germany/Museumslandschaft Hessen Kassel/ Ute Brunzel), 39 (Birmingham Museums and Art Gallery), 40 (National Gallery, London, UK), *contents page* and 41 (Private Collection), 43 (Regensburg Museum, Regensburg, Germany/Interfoto), *contents page detail*, 40 *detail* and 45 (Burrell Collection, Glasgow, Scotland/© Glasgow City Council, Museums), 48 (Private Collection), 52 (British Museum, London, UK); Corbis: 42 (Patrick Ward), 58 (Franz-Marc Frei); Ronald Grant: 9 (courtesy Warner Bros/Seven Arts), 21 (courtesy New Line Cinema); Kobal Collection: 13 (Columbia), 15 (MGM), 18 (TNT/WB/Holtz, George), 23 (Paramount), 31 (Artistes Associés/PEA); Rex Features: 36 (Alastair Muir), 37 (James Fraser), *title page* and 54 (Ray Roberts), 55 (ITV), 59 (Everett Collection); Topfoto: 5 and 50 (Charles Walker), 8 and 48 *detail* (Alinari), 12 (Print Collector/HIP), 22, 24 (Print Collector/HIP), 27 (Ellie Kurtz/RSC/ARPL), 28 (Roger Viollet), 30 (ARPL), 33, 32 *detail* and 38 (British Library/HIP), 44 (Ullstein), 46 (British Library/HIP), 54 *detail* and 57 (Fotomas); Victoria and Albert Museum: 29, 49, 51, 53, (V&A Images).

Contents

Introduction

The terms "medieval" or the "Middle Ages" can mean anything from the "Dark Ages" that followed the end of the Roman Empire in 476 CE to the late Renaissance. Where fashion is concerned, however, the most interesting era is roughly 1100 to 1460. In Britain, this was the period between the Norman invasion by William the Conqueror, Duke of Normandy, and the rise of the Tudors, including King Henry VIII. This book looks at costumes and different fashions that were popular among medieval men and women—from wealthy nobles to humble peasants. It describes materials that were used at the time and suggests ways to re-create a medieval look from modern fabrics and accessories.

Textiles were the mainstay of the Middle Ages. In addition to the hugely popular and widely available wool fabrics, there were imported luxuries such as silks, brocades, and damasks from the East.

The availability of these new commodities meant that by the end of the medieval era, members of the aristocracy, together with the emerging middle classes, were dressing more extravagantly than ever before. For peasants, however, their clothes—like their lives—continued much the same.

In this book, we focus on the period from 1340 to 1460: the clothing that people consider typically medieval. This is the period most frequently plundered by movies, TV, books, and art as the "all-purpose" medieval look. It's the most popular era for re-enactments, not just in plays and on screen but also in terms of pageants, medieval banquets, weddings, battle re-enactments, and even corporate team-building exercises. If you are seeking advice on how to dress as a medieval knight, an aristocratic lady, or a lord of the manor, look no farther—the answers are here.

THE ENGLISH CLOTH TRADE

In medieval England, certain towns began to specialize in particular trades. John Hooker, writing about the city of Exeter, in Devon, in 1575, noted that it had once been full of "clothiers and producers of broad cloths, destined primarily for Spain and southern Europe." In those days, he said, English broadcloth—a densely woven, felted wool cloth—was of such good quality that it was known all over Europe by the name of the town where it was made. By the time Hooker was writing, however, business had taken the place of craftsmanship: Exeter was now full of merchants and shopkeepers, "of whom the merchants are the most prominent and wealthiest."

The World of the Middle Ages

FEUDAL SOCIETY

At the beginning of the medieval period, most of Europe operated as a feudal society, organized in a pyramid structure. The king and queen were at the top, followed by the nobility, then knights, clergy, and commoners. The nobles lived in castles, while commoners grouped together in nearby villages. Other than London, large towns in Britain were as yet unknown. Almost everyone lived off the land: nobles hunted in the forests; commoners tended sheep, cattle, and poultry and grew a few crops.

There was a clear division between rich and poor and between gentry and country folk. There was also very little social mobility and not much interaction between the social classes. However, by the fourteenth century, a middle class was emerging, made up of merchants, bankers, tradesmen, and more sophisticated craftspeople. Before long, some of these people would be richer than their overlords.

Above: The nobles at this medieval feast emphasize their wealth and position by wearing rich, patterned fabrics and fur trimmed garments.

Left: Men's clothes might be any length between thigh and ankle, but women's garments were always floor length and often trailed on the ground.

PRACTICAL MATERIALS

The nobility of Europe may have reveled in expensive and exotic imported fabrics, but wool was the cloth most in demand. It was warm, took dye easily, and could be produced in weights to suit any number of garments, from the finest kirtle to a thick, felted winter cloak. Medieval folk did not have separate wardrobes for summer and winter but simply added another layer or a lining in cold weather.

Linen, made from the flax plant, was used for underwear and shirts. The best quality came from France and Flanders, but most ordinary people grew a little flax in the garden, from which they wove their own fabric. Cotton, not indigenous to Europe, had been introduced to Spain in the ninth century by Moors from North Africa, but it was not widely used other than as low-quality padding material. There is no real substitute for linen's versatility, and it is readily available today. However, fine cottons can be used as an alternative.

FASHION FROM THE EAST

Following the discovery of exotic Eastern fabrics during the Crusader period, trade routes to the Orient opened up, and a whole range of glamorous fabrics became available. The climate of the Middle East favored light materials, such as silk and gauzes, which were regarded as exotic luxuries in chillier Europe. Figured woven brocades and damasks were also immensely popular. These arrived in Europe via the Italian

Right: The foremost Italian families of the day, such as the Medici, had themselves painted in narrative scenes, wearing their finest clothes.

cities of Venice and Genoa, centers of trade along the Silk Road. However, local industries soon sprang up. Silk was produced all around the Mediterranean, but the highest quality came from Italy. While most of these fabrics are in common use today, the cost of "the real thing" is generally prohibitive. Cheaper, artificial fabrics offer a good alternative.

THE HEIGHT OF FASHION

Returning knights also brought news of how foreign nobles dressed. This gave rise to passing fads such as the wearing of Turkish-style gowns and turbans, but the long-term effect was the adoption of luxury fabrics and a general consciousness of style. The period after about 1340 was a highly fashion-conscious age. Trends changed rapidly: hemlines went up and down, sleeves brushed the floor, and hats threatened to topple over under their own height and weight. Fashion was driven, then as now, by the younger generation, and men seem to have been even more style-conscious than women.

Above: As Guinevere in the movie *Camelot*, Vanessa Redgrave wore a variety of costumes, some of which were purely medieval, while others resembled the flowing drapery of Botticelli paintings.

FASHION STARS OF FRANCE

Philip the Bold liked to parade his whole court in costumes of red and pale green, the colors of his house. These "were made of velvet and silk for the nobility and of satin and serge for the servants." When Philip the Good rode to Paris alongside the Dauphin (later Louis XI), not only his own clothes but his horse's trappings were so beautiful and so covered in rubies and diamonds that "beside it the clothes of the heir to the French throne looked almost pitiful."

Although tailoring as we know it was still unheard of, garments were no longer simply straight-seamed and draped. They fit better and revealed more of the body. The court of the dukes of Burgundy—known as "the most voluptuous and splendid court in Europe"—took over from the Italian city-states in setting the fashion throughout Europe for what noblemen and noblewomen should wear. Illustrations of the period show elegant, rich people relaxing in gardens, wearing fur-trimmed silk and velvet gowns in brilliant colors.

THE LONG AND SHORT OF IT

Throughout history, the length of a person's clothing has been a sure indication of wealth, partly because fabric was so expensive and partly because impractical clothing showed that you did not need to work. Nobles wore clothes at ankle length; peasants were content with a tunic that reached the thigh. At the beginning of the fourteenth century, there was little distinction between male and female clothing: nobles wore long, flowing, or pleated robes with an overtunic or cloak and a hat or cap. Later in the period, from the 1340s onward, younger men began to show off their shapely legs in short tunics cut to the hip and colored stockings, a fashion led by the Italians. But since even upper-class homes still had

Textiles were often named after their major center of production. Damask was "cloth from Damascus" in Syria, muslin came from Mosul in Iraq, and gauze came from the Palestinian city of Gaza. Taffeta, a crisp, smooth woven silk, comes from the Persian *taftan* ("to shine"). Tabby, a kind of striped taffeta, is named after al-Attabiya, a district of Baghdad. The wonderfully named musterdevillers was a gray cloth, named after a town in Normandy. "Cloth of Tars" was from Tartary. Other names come from the fabric's color: "murrey" was a purple-red cloth the color of mulberry, russet a reddish brown homespun fabric, and scarlet a thick, felted wool, dyed bright red.

Above: Chaucer reads *The Canterbury Tales* to an audience. This nineteenth-century version of medieval costume shows a variety of detail, including dagging and a liripipe hood (bottom right).

no glazing or heating, warmth remained an important consideration. Finer fabrics meant more layers of clothing, while linings and trimmings, especially fur, came into their own.

REFLECTING THE AGE

By the late fourteenth century, the scene was changing. More towns were springing up, many of them built on the cloth and clothing trades. The two great literary works of late-fourteenth-century England, Geoffrey Chaucer's *The Canterbury Tales* and William Langland's *Piers Plowman*, offer a vibrant, gossipy cross section of medieval society, and both describe their characters' clothing in great detail, leaving us in no doubt that costume was a sure indicator of class, wealth, and status.

RE-CREATING THE LOOK

The Middle Ages is a fascinating era, not just for its elegance but because of the growing appreciation of traditional crafts and handmade things. It is also the first period for which we have real pictorial evidence. Illuminated manuscripts, Books of Hours, and calendars all show, in jewel-like colors and in great detail, the fashions and the activities of the time. A Book of Hours was a collection of devotional texts for each hour of the day (hence the name), used by non-clergy people. Highly illustrated with biblical scenes alongside those of contemporary everyday life, these books were prized and available only to the rich. Jean, Duc de Berry, son of the king of France, commissioned five books for his own use, the most famous of which is *Très Riches Heures du Duc de Berry* (1413).

These are the best source of information for costume researchers. It is interesting to compare these illustrations—made at the time and therefore more reliable—with some of the costumes created for movies set in the medieval period. Clearly, many designers working in the movies have taken liberties with the clothing of the day. But however odd or laughable some of the re-creations are, they are fascinating—and welcome—for the effect they have had in inspiring people's interest in the medieval period.

Below: The illustration for the month of July from this Book of Hours (1490) shows peasants harvesting wheat in lightweight summer costume.

CHAPTER 2

What My Lady Wore

> *One was clothed in a kerchief*
> *clustered with pearls*
> *which shone like snow—snow on*
> *the slopes*
> *of her upper breast and bright bare*
> *throat.*
> *The other was noosed and knotted*
> *at the neck,*
> *her chin enveloped in chalk-white*
> *veils,*
> *her forehead fully enfolded in silk*
> *with detailed designs at the edges*
> *and hems.*

Anonymous, *Sir Gawain and the Green Knight*, c.1400

KIRTLE AND GOWN

Throughout the medieval period, women's clothing in Europe consisted of a one-piece gown, or kirtle, worn over a basic linen smock, an overtunic of some kind, and a head covering, which at various times might be a hood, a veil and circlet, or a crown (not confined to queens). Although there were many changes in detail, these basic elements remained the same.

In the twelfth and thirteenth centuries, the kirtle hung loose to the floor but was quite close-fitting and not yet gathered into folds or pleats. An overtunic, with wide sleeves, went over it, and sometimes a cloak was worn over the whole. Generally without hoods and front openings, cloaks were pulled on over the head and arranged in folds. The hair was worn in very long braids, sometimes with the addition of false hair, which hung forward over the shoulders. Unmarried women left their heads uncovered; an older woman might wear a veil and circlet.

Right: This is the costume of a well-to-do woman from the reign of Edward III (1327–77). She is wearing a cotehardie with wide hanging sleeves lined with contrasting silk.

Above: Audrey Hepburn in the movie *Robin and Marian* shows how the wimple was worn and how it was adopted by nuns as part of the habit.

MAKE IT—A BARBET AND FILLET

Take two strips of fine white linen or gauze about an inch wide and 18 inches long. Pass the first one (the barbet) under your chin, in front of the ears, and pin it on top of your head. Wrap the second (the fillet) around the forehead and secure it to the chin band at the points where they cross. This is a base for veils, which can be pinned at the front. Those with long hair can wear it with a snood.

By the late thirteenth century, the gown was more voluminous and worn with a girdle to catch in the fullness. "Magyar" sleeves, cut in a piece with the body of the gown, were popular.

EARLY HEAD COVERINGS

A popular head covering was the barbet and fillet. The barbet was a band of linen passed under the chin and pinned on top of the head, while the fillet was a linen circlet that went around the temples. This could be worn with a veil, with a snood to hold the hair, or with a wimple, popular in the twelfth century and worn until much later by older women. The wimple was a fine linen scarf, arranged to cover the neck and then, with the ends drawn up and tied on top of the head, to frame the face. It was usually covered with a veil or, later, a hat. Hair was rarely seen, which is a bonus when trying to conceal twenty-first-century haircuts.

STYLE REVOLUTION

From 1340, women's clothing fell into two very distinct styles. In the early years, the kirtle narrowed to a long, smooth, body-hugging single garment known as a cotehardie. The bodice fit tightly to the hips, then flowed into generous folds, often extending into a long train. It was worn with a girdle, slung low on the hips, which tied at the front and whose ends sometimes reached the floor. The neckline was often wide and low, leaving the shoulders bare, and the sleeves were narrow, buttoned, or sewn from elbow to wrist. Very often, additional hanging sleeves, or tippets, were attached just above the elbow. From here they hung in various lengths, often right down to the floor.

The cotehardie was very similar to the garment worn by men of the same period, but for women it was always worn long. A sideless overtunic or surcoat went over it. This was usually waist or hip length and edged with fur.

Below: Necklines could be high or, as shown here, wide and low. The lady in blue has bells sewn onto her dress. Note the extraordinary variety of hats and hoods being worn!

STYLE TIP

Medieval outfits were generally made up of several layers. Since only parts of these—usually sleeves or the neckline—were visible, it's possible to cheat a little and avoid making two whole garments. For example, a plain-colored, long-sleeved T-shirt with a line of fancy buttons sewn along the underarm gives you the close-fitting undersleeves of a woman's cotehardie.

Above: Elizabeth Taylor in the 1952 movie *Ivanhoe*: her costume is fairly accurate, although white was not usually worn. Note the guards in the background, with their leather tunics and jerkins.

Clearly, these outfits demand a little more sewing skill than the earlier straight tunics. However, patterns are available in books and on many dedicated Web sites, and the sewing is still relatively simple, based on straight widths of fabric and triangles. Triangular gores of fabric let into the side seams give the required fullness of a simple cotehardie.

SEWN INTO YOUR CLOTHES

Illustrations suggest that gowns were laced from neck to waist at the back or sometimes in front, but some historians believe that given the limits of tailoring, some of these close-fitting garments may have been actually sewn in place on the wearer. Certainly it's possible that the tight-fitting

FUR

The most popular fur came from a squirrel that was blue-gray on the back with a white underside. The fur was known as vair (gray) and miniver (white) and could be sewn together in alternating patterns. Ermine, the winter fur of the stoat, was worn only by royalty. When sewn together, the white coat and black tail give an impression of black spots on white. In 1406, the trousseau of Princess Philippa, daughter of Henry IV, included "a hood of scarlet cloth and a hood of black cloth, both furred with miniver," and "a cap of beaver furred with ermine garnished with a silk button and tassel."

sleeves of a cotehardie may have been achieved in this way. Today's stretch fabrics, such as velour, side-step this problem and are ideal for this style of garment.

THE HOUPPELANDE

The other style, popular from about 1360, could not have been more different. The voluminous houppelande, which originated in the Netherlands, featured a huge amount of material gathered into heavy folds by a high belt and had wide, hanging sleeves and either a high, stand-up collar or a V-neck. Cut from four panels, it had seams at the front, back, and sides, which were sometimes left unstitched at the lower part as vents. The edges of sleeves, hem, and vents were often trimmed with an embroidered panel or with fur or decorated with dagging. Some later versions of the houppelande buttoned right down the front. By about 1400, the houppelande had replaced the gown and cotehardie for women of any substance. By the late fifteenth century, however, a new

Right: You can see from these velvet houppelandes just how much fabric went into them. Note also the variety of sleeves that are worn.

STYLE TIP

These days, furnishing fabric is a good substitute for the large-patterned medieval fabrics. It also gives the required weight and "hang." For a cheaper version, it's possible to create these figured materials by stenciling with spray paint. However, both fabric paint and fabric inks need to be heat-set before the fabric is used. This is done by ironing over the design (covered with a pressing cloth) for two minutes with the iron on a high setting and steam off. For better results, repeat on both sides.

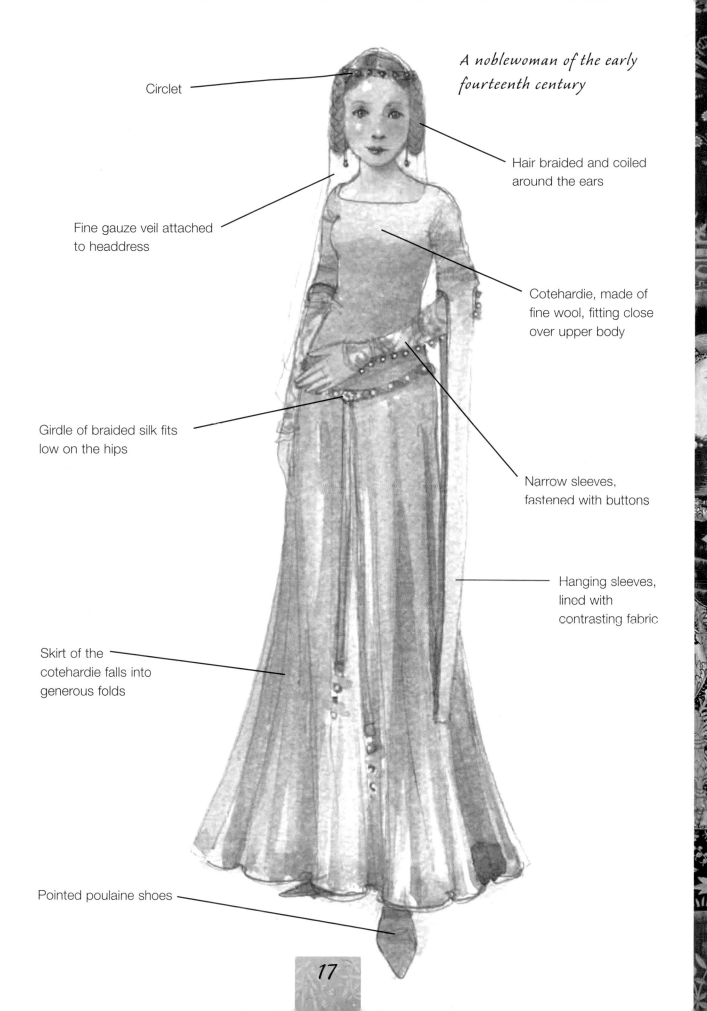

Circlet

Fine gauze veil attached
to headdress

Girdle of braided silk fits
low on the hips

Skirt of the
cotehardie falls into
generous folds

Pointed poulaine shoes

*A noblewoman of the early
fourteenth century*

Hair braided and coiled
around the ears

Cotehardie, made of
fine wool, fitting close
over upper body

Narrow sleeves,
fastened with buttons

Hanging sleeves,
lined with
contrasting fabric

Right: The 2001 TV movie *The Mists of Avalon*—another version of the King Arthur legend—had fairly authentic costumes but too much hair displayed.

EMBROIDERY

Embroidery was the most popular form of decoration for both ecclesiastical and secular clothing. Edward III of England established an embroidery workshop in the Tower of London. In 1351, he and his queen wore robes, almost certainly made there, of red velvet "embroidered with clouds of silver and eagles of pearl and gold, under each alternate cloud an eagle of pearl, and under each of the other clouds a golden eagle, every eagle having in its beak a Garter with the motto 'hony soyt qui mal y pense' [shame be to him who evil thinks] embroidered thereon."

fashion would combine the figure-revealing slimness of the cotehardie with the wide sleeves of the houppelande.

Whatever the style, women's clothing continued to be floor length. The hem of a houppelande might be as many as twelve yards around and often extended into a train. These were dresses of considerable stateliness.

FABRICS

To produce the overall impression of bulk and substance, the best clothes were made of heavy materials such as velvet, brocade, silk, or damask, all imported from the East via Italy or France. They were woven or stamped, usually with very large repeat patterns of flowers and foliage, often featuring exotic fruits such as pomegranates and artichokes, which betray their Eastern origins. Today, furnishing fabrics are a good substitute since they not only give the required "hang" but also employ very similar patterns. Small patterned fabrics are to be avoided as are light, slippery ones—the silks of the medieval period were heavy and textured. Furnishing velvet, although it sometimes lacks the rich pile of better-quality fabric, is always useful. Furnishing braid is also good to use.

Geometric designs, checks, and stripes were considered elegant. If not actually woven into the fabric, the effect of checks and stripes could be achieved by patchworking pieces of colored fabric together. With napped fabrics such as velvet, and especially with fur, setting alternate panels upside down or brushing the pile in different directions produced a shaded effect. This is very useful today in achieving these effects at little cost.

Left: Collectors' costume dolls wear historical dress made in modern fabrics. This patterned brocade is typical of the medieval period.

COLORS

Colors tended to the bright and cheery for the young, especially red, bright green, and blue, while rich russets, brown, and black were worn by the older generation. The popularity of red, green, blue, and gold—the colors of heraldry—is not surprising, given the importance of heraldry in society at large. It was also the origin of the craze for particolored clothing—the two halves of a tunic or hose in contrasting colors—which recalled the painted lozenges on the surcoats of crusading knights. However, colors depended on the availability of dyes, and while many of the plant-based ones were freely available, some—such as saffron for yellow and the crushed shells of seasnails for purple—were prohibitively expensive. Colors are a minefield for the costumer, and it goes almost without saying that characters should always be dressed according to their status.

NECKLINES

The most common style of houppelande had a deep V-neck front and back, often extending right down to the belt and revealing a contrasting fabric underneath. In some cases, this would have been the smock, but

Above: Victorian medievalist painters created fantasies of fabric and color. However, sometimes the costume research went astray: these necklines are too low, and ermine (the white, spotted fur) was worn only by the monarch and the highest aristocracy.

illustrations suggest that separate panels of rich fabric may have been sewn in to fill the gap. Certainly this is a good alternative today to avoid too many layers of fabric.

Another version of the houppelande was buttoned high at the throat into a funnel shape but the top buttons were left undone, creating a collar that stood high above the shoulders and arched over. A third followed the same shape but, made in softer material, turned over into a flat collar that lay wide across the shoulders.

SLEEVES

As with necklines, there were many variations on the sleeve, which came and went according to fashion. Some were quite plain; the same width from shoulder to wrist, they ended in a trim of fur or embroidery. "Bagpipe" sleeves, popular around 1400 to 1430, were very loose and full but gathered into a cuff at the wrist. The most popular and long-lasting fashion, however, was for huge funnel-shaped sleeves that hung to the floor, revealing the narrow, fitted sleeve of the undergarment. This style persisted much longer in women's garments than in men's.

UNDERWEAR

History tells us that a plain linen smock was still the only garment worn under whichever style was in fashion. Other than this, and knee-length hose, underwear for women was unknown. However, the full-bosomed look seen in illustrations is quite hard to achieve without some kind of

structuring. While today's costume designers believe that wearing modern underwear under historical clothing ruins the "look," wearers usually differ.

CROWNING GLORIES

Religious teaching dictated that most women keep their heads covered, either with a hat, a hood, or a veil. Because of this, the hairstyles beneath are hard to define, but it seems likely that hair was worn braided and looped up around the ears. In many cases, women shaved their hairline to give a high forehead and prevent hair from straggling out from under its covering. Hair was only revealed and worn loose by unmarried girls, by queens at their coronation, and by brides, who crowned it with a wreath of flowers. Between about 1400 and 1450, hats became very elaborate.

WOMEN AT HOME

Illustrations of the period suggest that the domestic occupations of upper-class women were limited to decorative embroidery or small-scale weaving, which is true to some extent. However, many of these women were very capable and held positions of power. Many headed religious institutions as abbesses or prioresses; others ran households while husbands were away at war or on business. They were also the ones who wrote diaries and kept up family correspondence, from which we can gather many details about clothing.

Above: Because *The Lord of the Rings* was set in a fantasy medieval world, it was allowed a few design liberties. Cate Blanchett, as the elfin Galadriel, wears a dress closely modeled on the cotehardie but made in a very un-medieval see-through fabric.

AS NATURE INTENDED

"Fair daughters, see that you pluck not away the hairs from your eyebrows nor from your temples nor from your foreheads, to make them appear higher than Nature ordained."

Knight de la Tour-Landry, advice to his daughters, c.1371

CHAPTER 3

What the Lord of the Manor Wore

THE EARLY PERIOD

Early male dress consisted of a straight tunic, slightly fitted in the bodice and widening into a skirt, worn knee or calf length except by the nobility on ceremonial occasions and by old men. Necklines were round with a vertical slit and edged with embroidery for the more sophisticated. Sleeves were straight and fairly close-fitting. A sleeveless overtunic, decorated with bands of embroidery at neck, hem, and wrist, went over this. All these are easy to make because they can be cut from straight pieces of cloth and do not involve curved seams or fitting. Braies, or loose breeches, went underneath. The cloak worn over all this might be rectangular, fastened across the chest by a chain and/or brooch. This demands virtually no sewing other than hemming. Almost as simple is the semicircular version, cut from a single piece of cloth. This was thrown over one shoulder and secured by a brooch or pin.

Above: In this early version of the King Arthur legend, the figure on the right wears a slit overtunic. The man on the left wears his hood spread over his shoulders like a cape.

Above: Peter O'Toole (left) and Richard Burton in the 1964 movie *Becket*, set around 1160. The silk tunics are suitably simple in cut and fabric, but medieval garments would not have had inset sleeves like this.

A NEW STYLE

The thirteenth-century fashion for Magyar sleeves was taken up in a big way by men. It consisted of a wide, deep armhole almost to the waist, with the sleeve itself narrowing to a cuff. Both floor- and calf-length gowns were slit up to the waist. A new hooded garment called the herygoud appeared. Pulled on over the head, it had long hanging sleeves with a slit at elbow level for the hands to pass through. This arrangement of hanging sleeves would last well into the Renaissance period. Hoods and hats were invariably worn.

THE COTEHARDIE ARRIVES . . .

From about 1340, men's clothing followed the same pattern as women's. The long tunic gave way to the shorter jupon—what would later be called a doublet. Padded and quite fitted, it was laced or buttoned down the

Right: The man on the left is in a full-length houppelande with an exaggeratedly high collar and dagged sleeves, while the other has dagged every edge of his clothing from sleeves to hem.

front. Over this went the male version of the cotehardie, a belted coat fitted to the waist, then flaring into a full skirt, open at the front and reaching to the knee. The sleeves were narrow to the elbow, where they fell into a deep hanging flap.

. . . FOLLOWED BY THE HOUPPELANDE

Just as voluminous as the woman's version, the man's houppelande was worn belted at the natural waist. The seams, at the front, back, and each side, were left open as vents, frequently as high as the waist. The sleeves fell into huge funnels at the wrist and often trailed on the ground. The houppelande was always lined, usually with fur, and normally trimmed. Edges and hems were often cut into wavy shapes called daggets. Unlike the woman's version, however, the houppelande could be worn long—mainly on ceremonial occasions—or at any length between knee and calf. This versatility kept it popular well into the fifteenth century.

RAISING THE HEMLINE

By the second half of the fourteenth century, the skirts of the jupon and the cotehardie had both become daringly short, especially on younger men eager to show off their elegant legs. Padding and quilting across the chest enhanced the manly appearance. This fashion originated in Italy

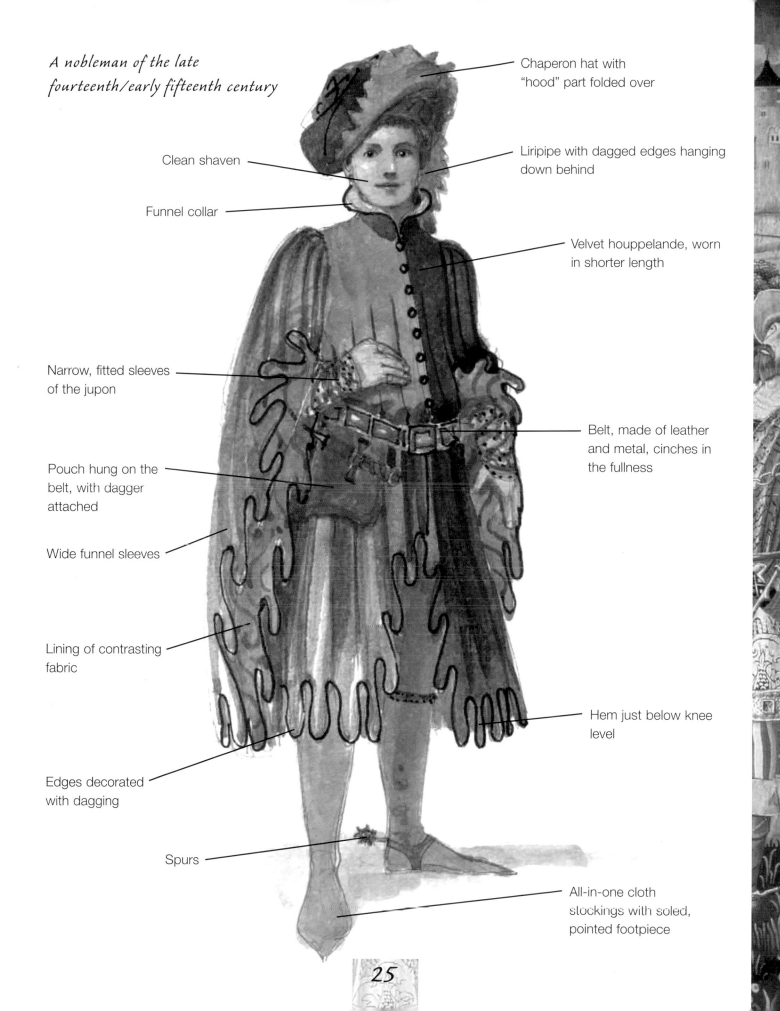

A nobleman of the late fourteenth/early fifteenth century

Clean shaven

Funnel collar

Chaperon hat with "hood" part folded over

Liripipe with dagged edges hanging down behind

Velvet houppelande, worn in shorter length

Narrow, fitted sleeves of the jupon

Pouch hung on the belt, with dagger attached

Wide funnel sleeves

Belt, made of leather and metal, cinches in the fullness

Lining of contrasting fabric

Hem just below knee level

Edges decorated with dagging

Spurs

All-in-one cloth stockings with soled, pointed footpiece

Right: The Italians were the first to shorten the tunic. The rigid pillbox hat worn by these young men is also very typical of this period in Italy but is not seen much elsewhere.

and spread quickly through Europe. For this style, less dependent on "hang," fabrics are lighter. Silk comes into its own, replacing the heavier brocades. Silk lining material can be used here, although very shiny fabrics should be avoided.

DAGGING

This form of decoration was very popular between about 1380 and 1450. The edges of garments—hems, vents, the wide sleeves, collars—were cut deeply into scallops, leaves, or tongues. The ultra-fashionable took this expression of style to extremes. Sometimes the vents in the skirt of a garment were left unstitched as high as the chest and the edges dagged, so that the panels looked like broad ribbons of fabric, floating as the wearer moved. When cut around the stand-up collar of a houppelande, dagging gave the appearance of an early ruff. A word of warning here: dagging should be used sparingly to avoid a comic effect.

THE PEACOCK MALE

In Italy and Burgundy, and to a lesser extent in England, men's fashion outshone that of women, with the same silks, damasks, and velvets dominating their wardrobes. Men were not afraid of patterns and colors,

and contrasting linings made cloaks and overgarments even more decorative. On the whole, the impression of richness is in the material and its pattern rather than in laid-on decoration. Curious and extreme fashions for hose, featuring legs of different colors, and other particolored garments or elaborate hats, usually originated in Italy. However, Italy was more than just the home of eccentricity. The Medici family in Florence represented not only the high point of Italian fashion in the fifteenth century but also the supreme example of clothing as an indication of power and influence.

CHEATING

Although the visible parts of an outfit were made of fine fabric, cheaper material was used for those parts that would be covered by other garments, especially the back. The same applied to linings and interlinings put in for warmth, which were often made of thick blanket cloth. This is a good rule of thumb for modern costumers, too—what can't be seen need not cost much.

WHAT'S UNDERNEATH

It's important to make a distinction between braies, or breeches, which essentially cover the loins, and hose, which are coverings for the legs. For a long time, these remained quite separate articles. The earliest braies look something like a baggy Indian *dhoti* (loincloth) but gradually separated into loose drawers, held up by a drawstring just below the waist. Cutoff pajama pants are the nearest approximation today and are certainly more comfortable. Cloth stockings with feet, cut on the cross and sewn up the back, reached up each thigh and were tied on the outside

Below: This parade of fashionable young men shows them wearing one-piece footed hose instead of shoes. The tunics, especially the tabard-style ones on the left, are just long enough to cover the top of the hose. No wonder people were shocked!

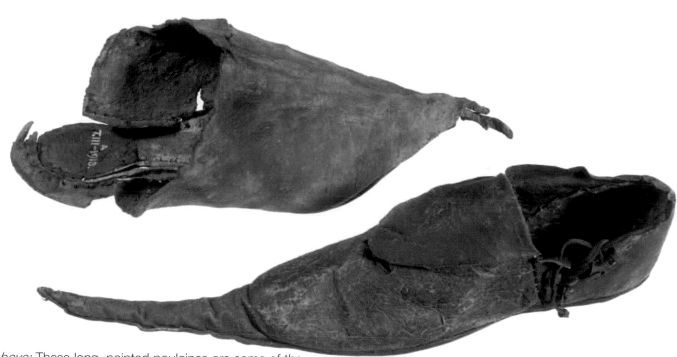

Above: These long, pointed poulaines are some of the very few items of medieval clothing to have survived. You can even see the tie at the side.

of the leg to the braies. However, as the jupon—and, consequently, the braies—got shorter, the hose got longer until they had to be attached to the doublet itself by means of points, or laces. From here it was only a matter of time—around 1390—before the two legs were joined at the center into what we would recognize as a pair of tights. For strict historical accuracy, separate legs of hose can be made, but in general, colored tights are perfectly acceptable.

FOOTWEAR

Boots were worn for walking and for riding; shoes varied in style but on the whole were flat, long, and pointed. Some were fastened with buckles, others with lacing up the instep, somewhat in the style of today's stretch flats (which make a good modern alternative). Hose were also soled with leather and worn without shoes: this was not just a poor man's alternative but a fashionable one. Sometimes the feet of the hose were stuffed with straw or moss to achieve the pointed look, known as pikes.

COVERING YOUR HEAD

Hats came in great variety, many of them worn on top of the basic coif or hood. Men were rarely seen bareheaded. From the thirteenth century, men wore their hair waved to the nape of the neck, with a center parting and bangs. Young men favored bobbed hair with a rolled curl across the

SIR JOHN'S WARDROBE

The wardrobe accounts of aristocratic families are a good source of information. The account of Sir John Fastolf reveals that in 1459 he had four jackets. One was in blue velvet, the body lined with linen and the sleeves with blanket cloth; another, in red velvet, had the vents bound with red leather. A third was more showy, with the front and sleeves of black velvet, the rest of russet wool. The last, of soft deerskin, had the neck edged with black velvet. Of his gowns, one was of cloth of gold and one of blue velvet, lined and trimmed with fur. He also had three wool gowns, one in red, lined with rabbit fur, one of green wool, and one of scarlet.

The male version of the houppelande, later the "uniform" of the Elizabethan medical profession, lasted down the centuries and eventually became the academic gown that is worn today. It is still recognizable by its fullness and deep, bell-like sleeves. Academic hoods, too, although worn only across the shoulders rather than on the head, retain their brightly colored silk linings, fur trimming, and, in some universities, even a liripipe.

Right: Prince Henry the Navigator of Portugal is wearing his hood with a long liripipe hanging over his shoulder. At least the hood is a good, plain black: many of these dangling points were very ornate.

forehead. John Gower, writing of a man about town in his *Confessio Amantis*, mentions his "well-combed croquet-curl." The long, forked beards of the previous age had gone, along with the shaggy hair, but moderate beards and mustaches were fashionable. Mustaches without beards were rarely seen.

SUMPTUARY LAWS

All this extravagance was clearly getting out of hand. According to Henry Knighton, in his *Chronicle* (1337–96): "There was so much pride amongst the common people in vying with one another in dress and

Left: Pier Paolo Pasolini's movie version of Chaucer's *The Canterbury Tales* (1972) was an unorthodox view of the Middle Ages, as we can see from these strange costumes. They seem to combine the medieval world with that of the cowboy.

ornament that it was scarcely possible to distinguish the poor from the rich, the servant from the master, or the priest from any other man."

Sumptuary laws regulated the wearing of certain clothing and were intended largely to curb extravagance and to discourage extreme fashions among the upper classes. However, they also served to perpetuate a social hierarchy in which everybody knew his or her place and stayed in it. The sumptuary laws varied throughout Europe, but typical examples stated that the bourgeoisie were not permitted to wear multicolored, striped, or checked gowns, brocade or figured velvet, or fabrics embroidered with silver or gold thread. People could buy only a certain number of costumes per year, ranging from four for a territorial lord to three for a knight and just one for boys and young women below a certain income. Anyone seriously attempting to re-create medieval fashion should beware—contravening these laws was punishable by a heavy fine and/or forfeiture of the garments concerned, severe beating, or even death.

A POINT OF LAW

"No knight under the estate of a lord, esquire or gentleman, nor any other person, shall wear any shoes or boots having pikes or points exceeding the length of two inches, under the forfeiture of forty pence; and every shoemaker who shall make pikes for shoes or boots beyond the length stated in this statute shall forfeit for every offence the sum of forty pence. "
Sumptuary law of 1363

CHAPTER 4

Knights and Soldiers

DRESSING A KNIGHT

*"He tries on his tunic of
    extravagant silk,
then the neatly cut cloak,
    closed at the neck,
its lining finished with a layer
    of white fur.
Then they settled his feet in
    steel shoes
and clad his calves, clamped
    them with greaves,
then hinged and highly
    polished plates
were knotted with gold thread
    to the knight's knees.
Then leg-guards were fitted,
    lagging the flesh,
attached with thongs to his
    thick-set thighs.
Then comes the suit of
    shimmering steel rings
encasing his body and his
    costly clothes:
well burnished braces to both
    of his arms,
good elbow guards and
    glinting metal gloves,
all the trimmings and
    trappings of a knight tricked
    out to ride. "*

*Sir Gawain and the Green
Knight*, in a version by Simon
Armitage

Above: The armor worn at the Battle of Hastings in 1066, commemorated here in the famous Bayeux Tapestry, was a long hauberk made of chain mail.

MEN OF WAR

During the medieval period, warfare was a fact of life. The Norman invasion of England in 1066 changed the face of English society. The Crusades began in 1095 and lasted on and off until 1272, taking thousands of European men to the unknown lands of the Middle East to spread the Christian faith. The Hundred Years' War between England and France saw sporadic fighting all over France between 1337 and 1453. In Italy, the city-states were constantly at odds with one another. In England, the reigns of Richard II, Henry IV, and Henry VI were fraught with civil rebellion, culminating in the Wars of the Roses (1455–87). In addition to these major campaigns, there were local skirmishes between barons, for which tenants would regularly have to turn out and fight. These events have inspired dozens of movies, from the 1950s TV Crusader series *Ivanhoe* to the major Hollywood movie *El Cid* and versions of Shakespeare's *Henry V* by Laurence Olivier and Kenneth Branagh, not to mention innumerable productions of the other plays in Shakespeare's medieval history cycle, from *Edward III* to *Richard III*. The battles are also regularly re-enacted by serious historical societies on both sides of the Atlantic.

KNIGHTHOOD

The idea of the knight not just as a superior fighting machine but also as a member of a cultured, brotherly elite embodying the Christian virtues arose during the eleventh century and persisted until the end of the fifteenth century. At its height, during the thirteenth and fourteenth centuries, knighthood inspired chivalry, good manners, idealism, and the art of courtly love. It was the dominant socializing ideal of the period, and the knight is perhaps the most iconic figure in medieval history.

KING OF CAMELOT

The most famous knights in history, whether or not they really existed, are those of King Arthur's court at Camelot. The tales of Arthur and Guinevere, Lancelot, Gawain, and the rest were already ancient—and popular throughout Europe—when Thomas Mallory wrote them down in the late fourteenth century. In the nineteenth century, England underwent a popular revival of medievalism. Architects designed mock-Gothic buildings, poets such as Keats and Tennyson revived the Arthurian legends, and artists of the Pre-Raphaelite Brotherhood illustrated them in hundreds of paintings. Their wives, sisters, and mothers took up embroidery and tapestry depicting knights and ladies. The more bohemian among them took to wearing

Right: The 2004 movie *King Arthur* claimed specifically to be set in the year 467, but critics spotted several anachronisms, including a kind of crossbow not in popular use until the eleventh century. At least Clive Owen, here seen as Arthur, is using a sword.

The idea that fully armed knights had to be lifted onto their horses with the help of winches and pulleys is a myth! It gained currency through a comic scene in Mark Twain's novel *A Connecticut Yankee in King Arthur's Court* and the movie that followed, in which a bewildered, time-traveling American finds himself back in medieval Camelot. Required to go on a knightly quest, he first looks helplessly at the unfamiliar armor he's supposed to wear—not surprising when you look at the number of different pieces— and then has to be hoisted onto his horse. A good movie moment: a shame about the facts!

Right: These knights kneeling in prayer are from the late medieval period and are almost completely encased in steel armor. During the sixteenth century, plate armor started to become obsolete.

homemade medieval-style dresses. Many of the movies seen today take their inspiration from these secondhand re-creations, perpetuating their well-meaning inaccuracies.

THE KNIGHT'S CLOTHING

What knights really wore depended on whether they were seriously at war, performing in a tournament, or at home. Chaucer's knight, albeit "a perfect gentil knight," is depicted quite plainly: "He was not gaily dressed. / He wore a fustian tunic stained and dark / With smudges where his armour had left mark."

Perhaps the greatest ceremony of a knight's life was the ritual of clothing him for his oath-taking. It came when, after a night spent in prayer and fasting, he was bathed and then dressed in fine new garments. Ballads describe what he wore. The underclothing consisted of a long-sleeved shirt and braies of fine linen. Over this went a silk tunic that reached to somewhere between thigh and knee, then various items of metal armor. Depending on the period, some of these might be of chain

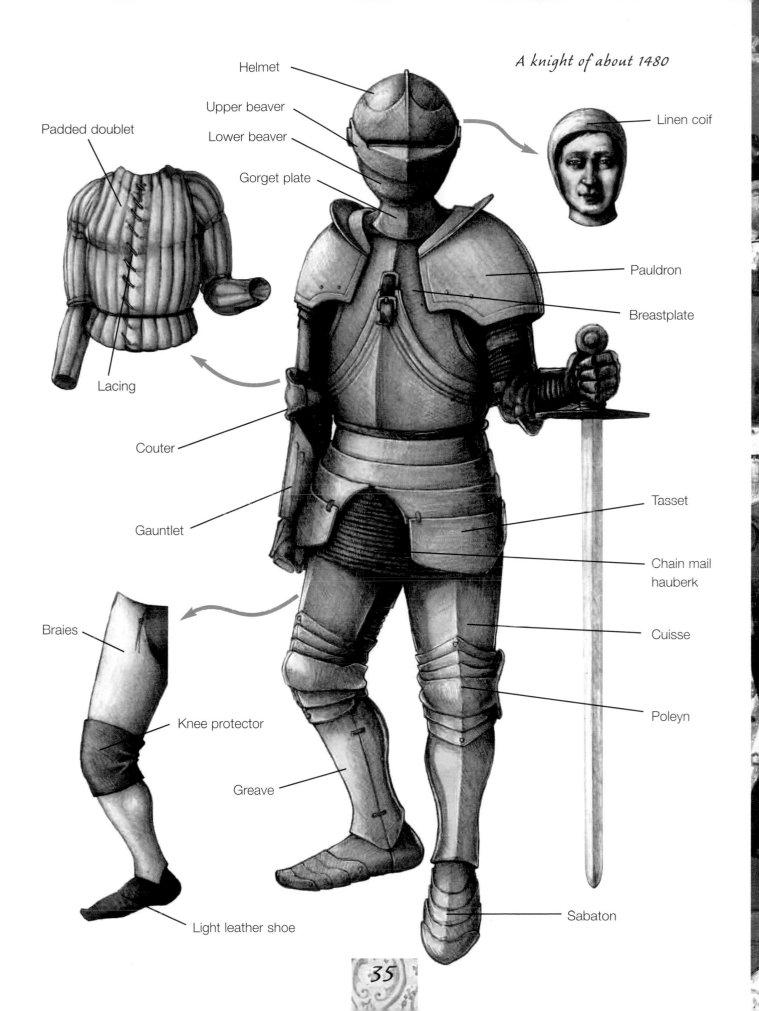

Helmet

Upper beaver

Lower beaver

Gorget plate

Padded doublet

Lacing

Couter

Gauntlet

Braies

Knee protector

Greave

Light leather shoe

A knight of about 1480

Linen coif

Pauldron

Breastplate

Tasset

Chain mail
hauberk

Cuisse

Poleyn

Sabaton

mail, and some of solid metal. He was then "dubbed," tapped on the shoulder with a sword, given his full title—"Sir Something of Somewhere"—and awarded his spurs.

ARMOR

Styles of armor changed a good deal during the medieval period. Serious battle re-enactment demands careful research into armor, but even for general purposes it's important to ensure that you combine the right elements. The twelfth-century knight was covered from shoulder to knee by a hooded tunic, or hauberk, of tiny interlocking metal rings known as chain mail. This was lined with fabric and sometimes padded for comfort. It's possible to replicate chain mail today, but it is specialist work. Loose knitting in thick cotton yarn or string, sprayed with metallic paint, is a far easier alternative.

As weaponry advanced, however, chain mail gave way to plate armor, which provided better protection from the arrows of the dreaded longbow. Beginning as individual plates buckled on over mail to protect

Below: The musical *Spamalot* was a great medieval spoof by the Monty Python team. The castle may look more like Disneyland than Camelot, but the knights are surprisingly authentic.

Above: Present-day re-enactors take their history seriously, even down to the creation of their coat of arms, which is repeated on the caparisons worn by the horses.

forearms and legs, plate armor gradually expanded to cover the whole body. The most prized armor, engraved with fine decoration and made in Germany, Flanders, and Italy, was worn only for tournaments and ceremonial occasions. Although it was not as unwieldy or heavy as one might think, by the late 1400s, wearers would have been hot and sweaty.

If you are dressing as a knight, spray-painted cardboard is by far the simplest and most comfortable option to suggest plate armor. Papier-mâché or plastic foam details can be glued on by the more ambitious. However, few knights wore full armor all the time, even on campaign. Armor can be suggested by just a few items on shoulders, forearms, and knees and with the addition of a helmet.

IDENTIFYING MARKS

Once in the field or at a tournament, the knight's armor was covered by a silk or linen surcoat, a garment borrowed from the Saracens (Arabs). It was sewn or embroidered with a distinguishing device that, by the time a helmet obscured the entire face, was the only way a knight could be identified. The same device appeared on his shield and on any trapping or pennants (flags) attached to his horse.

Most knights wore the badge or insignia of the order to which they belonged. Others wore the livery of their overlord or their own family crest. Unless you are lucky enough to have your own coat of arms, real heraldry is best avoided: it's a complex business with obscure rules and imagery. However, a simple device is easily painted or stenciled—the

Right: The two knights jousting here are wearing full metal tournament armor. You can also see that the lords and ladies watching make quite a fashion parade.

JOAN OF ARC

Joan of Arc, a young peasant girl who claimed divine inspiration, led the French army to victory over the English during the Hundred Years' War. Throughout the campaign she wore men's clothing and armor, and later, when she was put on trial for witchcraft and heresy, this was one of the main charges against her. It was said to be "contrary to divine law, abominable to God, condemned and prohibited by every law," because it looked as if she were trying to achieve the status of a man. In those days, this was unthinkable. Joan of Arc was burned at the stake in 1431. Remember, when costuming, no pants for women—ever.

Knights Hospitaller, one of the most famous orders of knighthood, wore a white Maltese Cross on a black ground. It's fun, too, to invent a simple, perhaps punning, image based on your name.

SQUIRES

Squires were usually the younger sons of knights or the offspring of wealthy families, so this is a good role for younger members of the family in re-enactments. As boys of twelve or so, they wore simple tunics, wool hose, and leather shoes (or perhaps soled hose), but as they approached knighthood themselves, dress became more sophisticated. Chaucer's young squire, riding on pilgrimage alongside his knight, was in fashionable civilian dress: "Soft was his gown, the sleeves were long and wide; / He knew the way to sit a horse and ride." He would, of course, have no spurs attached: these are the ultimate badge of knighthood.

THE OFF-DUTY KNIGHT

The knight also had a peacetime role, serving as escort and general companion to his lord. He spent a good deal of his leisure time out hunting, not just for fun but as good tactical training for war. For this and other energetic pursuits, he wore a short tunic and hose. At home, the upper-class knight had an image to keep up. He was well dressed and presentable at all times in the same houppelande or jupon worn by any other minor noble. Velvet and silk featured as much in his wardrobe as in his lady's or the king's.

COURTLY LOVE

The art of courtly love, in which a knight swore undying love to his lady in a (probably) platonic relationship of adoration and service, was at the heart of this male-dominated society. He worshiped her from afar, wrote poems in her praise, and, once in her favor, dedicated his noble deeds to her. The exchange of tokens and gifts was crucial in this relationship, and the knight often went into a tournament wearing his lady's glove or handkerchief on his helmet. Appropriate behavior should, of course, be strictly adhered to in any re-enactment situation.

FOOT SOLDIERS

Because there were no standing armies, there was as yet no military uniform. Styles differed from one country to another, but foot soldiers can safely be dressed in a jerkin made of padded "leather" or several layers of canvas, with wool hose and short leather boots. The most protection foot soldiers could expect was a mail hauberk, some "boiled leather" knee pieces, and perhaps a metal chain attached to the outer sleeve to ward off sword slashes. Some characters might wear bits and pieces of discarded metal armor plundered from the battlefield.

Below: Painter Edward Burne Jones captured the essence of chivalry and courtly love and steeped himself in the literature of the period. However, the flowing robes worn by these women look more like Greek or Roman drapery than anything you'd find in a Book of Hours.

CHAPTER 5

What the Common People Wore

THE MIDDLE CLASS

The aristocracy may have dominated the medieval fashion scene, but they were greatly outnumbered by the "ordinary" folk of Europe. Although the term had not yet been invented, a bourgeoisie, or middle class, largely composed of merchants and bankers, was growing all over Europe.

Below: The famous Arnolfini portrait is of a wealthy merchant and his wife and shows them dressed in suitably rich but plain fabrics—a fur-trimmed velvet robe over a damask tunic for him with a plaited-straw hat and for her a voluminous houppelande-style gown, also trimmed and lined with fur, with a long train.

The bourgeoisie imitated the fashions of the aristocracy, even if they could not always afford to keep up with the fine fabrics and the frequent changes of style. Thus, a townswoman of some substance happily wore a houppelande or a cotehardie, whose impractical details, such as the trailing train or impossibly deep sleeves, were originally intended for a woman who did no work. This aspirational dressing-up inevitably laid them open to ridicule from observers, just as extreme farthingales would in the Elizabethan period. Elaborate hats and long pointed shoes, in particular, attracted such criticism. In *The Canterbury Tales*, Chaucer is scathing about social-climbing wives who dress better than they should.

By the 1400s, the average townsman would be wearing a knee-length houppelande with wide sleeves and a high collar, made of wool and perhaps dyed a deep russet. His wife would be wearing a modest V-necked houppelande with wide revers and narrow fitted sleeves. Gathered with a high buckled belt, it might be lifted in front to reveal an underskirt. On her head, she probably wore a cornette, the favorite headgear of married women of the urban middle class well into the sixteenth century. It was essentially an elaborate wimple, a large piece of starched white linen folded into peaks that resembled horns.

SUBSTITUTES FOR SILK

Although cloth merchants and their wives clearly had access to the silk and brocades they were importing, most ordinary people made do with wool cloth, the finer the better. To compensate for this, more subtle dyeing and the use of trimmings—dagging and edging with fur and embroidery—came into their own as economical ways of making clothes more showy. This should be remembered by all costumers today.

TRAVELERS

Although they didn't spend their lives outdoors in the way that peasants did, working townspeople certainly traveled and moved around more than the castle dwellers. When they did, they were also more likely to be on foot or on horseback than carried in a litter. Characters on a journey would wear cloaks, hoods, and boots chosen for warmth. Men's cloaks and hoods were almost always separate garments, the hood worn around the shoulders or head and often topped by a hat. Women had the option of a hooded cloak, but fur-lined mantles were the privilege of the aristocracy. Today's

Below: Chaucer's "Wife of Bath", on the other hand, is wearing a gown of similar design but in more everyday wool ("scarlet"). She's also wearing a traveling hat over her coif.

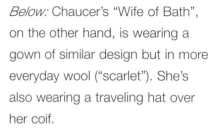

Above: Let's hope these "medieval" minstrels sound more authentic than they look! Guitars and wire-rimmed glasses were still a ways in the future.

"My mother sent to my father at London for a gown cloth of musterdevillers [a gray wool cloth] to make a gown for me. . . . I pray you, if it be not bought, that you will vouchsafe to buy it and send it home as soon as you may, for I have no gown to wear this winter but my black and my green . . . and that is so cumbrous that I am weary of it. As for the girdle that my father promised me . . . I pray you, if you will take it upon you, that you will vouchsafe to have it made before you come home, for I had never more need of it than now, for I have grown so slim that I cannot be girt into any girdle I have except one. "

Margaret Paston to her husband John, December 14, 1441

waterproof fabrics—gabardine, PVC, and so on—are not really usable here: medieval travelers just got wet.

BOOTS AND SHOES

Walking shoes were either fitted around the ankle or cut away over the instep and fastened by a buckled strap around the ankle. The more fashionable had holes punched into the front to form geometric patterns or flowers. Old-fashioned children's sandals, like those worn in the 1950s, are excellent equivalents. Boots for riding were either thigh length, fastened with laces or buckles at calf level, or knee length, loose and unshaped, fitted by a fold that was secured on the outside of the leg. A good alternative today is to wear sturdy shoes and then wrap separate buckled or laced leggings around the lower part of the leg to meet the shoes' uppers. By 1400, the vogue for pointed toes was taking hold, and boots and shoes had become slimmer-fitting, but remember that extravagant points are only for the wealthy.

WHO MADE THE CLOTHES?

Clothing for the better off was made by professional tailors. Like all craftspeople, they belonged to trade guilds. These were like trade unions, protecting the welfare and working conditions of their members and

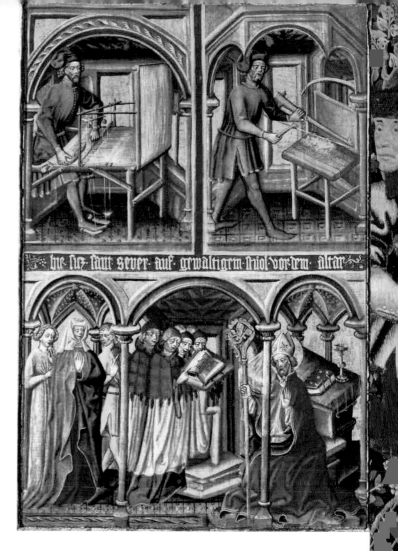

Right: This illustration of the medieval trade guilds shows workers engaged in the production of wool. The fine folk below are wearing the clothes the workers produce.

ensuring the quality of their work. They operated in conjunction with guilds of other, related tradesmen, such as drapers (cloth merchants) and haberdashers (traders in accessories and trimmings). Merchant guilds regulated prices and quality, policing weights and measures and general business practices in the town.

SERVANTS

In an aristocratic household, servants were simply but well dressed in order to reflect the status of their lord. However, illustrations of the period can be misleading: some servants who appear to be wearing an item of clothing that seems out of their class are probably dressed in their lord's livery or perhaps an out-of-fashion gift from their employer. While not exactly a uniform, livery was a way of distinguishing the members of the household. Servants in a noble house might wear the lord's badge sewn on their tunic or dress, while others just all wore the same color of clothing. This outfit was part of their salary: servants, and even quite senior officials, were given only one new outfit per year because they were so expensive.

A lady's maid benefited from her relationship to her mistress and might be given cast-off gowns. Kitchen maids and cooks were rarely seen by outsiders and did not warrant the expense of livery. They wore smocks and aprons, cut as low as possible to provide relief from the stifling heat of open fires and ovens. Outdoor workers, such as stable boys and gardeners, were likely to come into contact with visitors and so were better dressed. The knight's squire, neither a household servant nor yet a gentleman in his own right, was simply but neatly dressed in wool and linen. In company with his master, however, he would be more smartly attired.

COUNTRY FOLK

In almost every medieval manuscript illustration, rural peasants and agricultural workers can be seen scurrying about in the background, plowing, cutting corn, or shearing sheep. Peasant clothing, unlike that

FABRIC AND COLOR

Wool was the most popular fabric for clothing of all classes, not just because sheep were plentiful but because wool takes dye very well. Gowns, doublets (a man's close-fitting jacket), and most outer clothing could be produced in bright colors. Linen, on the other hand, is very difficult to dye and the colors fade quickly, so it was usually left white, making it more suitable for underclothing. Faded or yellowed linen could be brightened by leaving it out in the sun, where it turned white again.

Below: The man on the right has either rolled his hose down to knee level or is wearing half hose over his full-length pair. The objects hanging from the men's girdles are probably water bottles.

of their betters, changed hardly at all during the Middle Ages. Chaucer's plowman, for example, "wore a tabard smock and rode a mare." The old distinction of "long for the rich, short for the poor" persisted throughout, and as a general rule clothing was looser or more fitted depending on the degree of activity needed.

Men usually wore short wool tunics, wool hose, and ankle boots or flat shoes with rounded toes—no extravagant points here. To allow them greater freedom of movement, the tunic was sometimes tucked up into the belt and the hose rolled down to just above the knee and secured with a garter. Some men wore leather-soled hose. Poorer folk wore strips of linen or cotton wrapped around the leg and tied with crisscrossed twine. Few people were seen entirely bare-legged: appearing in this way was considered a mark of absolute poverty, and reflected an attitude that persisted throughout the Tudor and Elizabethan periods.

Calendars, or books describing the various labors suitable to each month of the year, show seasonal variations. In winter, wooden pattens kept the feet out of the mud. Broad-brimmed straw hats were worn in summer, their design hardly changing over centuries. Hoods and/or a wool cap of some kind—usually a beanie-style conical one—were always worn, with the weather, rather than fashion, in mind. Hardly anyone went bareheaded, but if they did, the hood was seen spread across the shoulders, ready to be pulled up. In the countryside, hooded cloaks were worn by both sexes.

Country folk made their own clothes. Most people grew flax for linen or hemp, used to make rope or a coarse, scratchy cloth. Many people also grazed sheep on the common land and spun and wove their own wool cloth. Spinning was women's work and done on a domestic basis, while most weavers were men.

DYEING FOR COLOR

Medieval dyeing was done in rudimentary fashion in pots over an
open fire, so subtlety of color was difficult to achieve. Bright primary
shades were much easier to produce, which explains why medieval
illustrations often show working people wearing brightly colored
clothing. Browns, grays, solid blacks, and pastels—much more difficult
to achieve—were the province of the aristocracy. Most dyes were made

Above: The walls of great
houses were hung with
tapestries depicting hunting or
country sports. Here people
are hunting rabbits with ferrets
and nets. Many are wearing
red, the color of huntsmen.

Right: Most of those involved in professional weaving, embroidery, or tapestry work, like these two, were men, although women did such things at a domestic level. The men are wearing aprons because they need to wipe their hands frequently in order to keep the thread free from sweat.

from plants growing freely in the countryside or garden, such as madder (red) and woad (indigo), and were accessible to all classes, although the very poor left their homespun "natural."

APRONS

These were worn by women of the middle and working classes and by tradesmen. They came in great variety and are a good way of distinguishing a character in a play or pageant. Those in messy jobs, such as butchers and fishmongers, wore full-length aprons that covered front and back, like a tabard. Cleaner jobs required only a half-length one, tied at the waist or with the upper corners simply tucked into the belt. Most women in domestic or agricultural work are seen wearing these. Farriers and stonemasons, in need of more protection, wore leather aprons, full length and tied behind the neck. Market women often wore a "bag apron," a useful garment that also served as a carrier. Aprons were also a badge of respectability among the less well off. Even if they could not afford a new gown, a clean white apron spruced up the old one and gave an impression of neatness. For housework, a rough apron went over the "best" white one.

Wide-brimmed hat

Linen coif

White linen shift

Laced bodice

Detachable sleeves

A working-class woman of the 1400s

Plain linen apron tied behind the back

Plain wool skirt, hitched up for working

Underskirt or shift

Drawstring pouch hanging from the girdle or attached inside skirt

Flat, pointed shoes

47

A SELECTION OF HOODS

According to his wardrobe inventory for 1459, Sir John Fastolf owned a number of elegant hoods. One was of russet velvet, lined with blue damask, with a parti-colored cape, half russet and half blue velvet. Another was made of scarlet (the cloth, not necessarily the color) set on a roll of purple velvet, and was edged with the same velvet. Others were of russet velvet, the cape lined with russet silk; purple velvet "without roll and tippet," and damask russet, the cape fastened with a silk lace.

CHAPTER 6

Hats, Hose, Girdles, and Gloves

MEDIEVAL ACCESSORIES

Because it was considered improper for married women to show their hair, wimples and coifs were popular throughout the period. A coif was a simple linen cap that covered the hair completely and framed the face. It was worn on its own or under a hat or hood. Coifs were worn by married women, by old men, and as nightcaps by both sexes. A wimple was a looser covering that extended to cover the chin and neck as well as the head. Made of fine linen or gauze, these could either be loose or starched to stand up in folds, sometimes supported by a wire frame.

HOODS . . .

The hood was the all-purpose accessory, worn by all classes in fabrics from wool to velvet. It resembled a loose balaclava (a knitted cap for the head and neck), extending into a cape over the shoulders and at the back into a point that, by the early 1300s, had grown into a long extension, or liripipe. This was worn hanging down the back or to one side, like a streamer—something of an affectation, especially when dagged—or coiled around the head like a turban. But by about 1400, hoods were being

Above: The astonishing variety of fashions in the medieval era is illustrated by differences in sleeves, necklines, trimmings, and, in particular, headgear.

Left: The round, felt "beanie"-style cap was one of the most popular. It could be worn set back on the head, as on this lovely painted tile, or at a rakish angle.

worn in completely new, and rather strange, ways. The face opening was pulled up to the forehead and the neck fabric rolled up into a brim. Alternatively, the opening could be fitted onto the head sideways and the neck flap and liripipe left hanging on either side or wrapped and folded in various ways on top of the head.

. . . AND HATS

The chaperon, the hat of choice throughout the mid-1400s, was a ready-made version of the hood-turban. A padded rope of fabric was sewn into a circle, sometimes twisted for further effect, and into this was sewn a loose "hood." The "hood" part could be worn standing up, flopping backward, forward, or sideways, or with liripipe attached, dagged or trimmed with bells. This type of accessory is easy to make.

Round felted caps, rather like a beret with a "stalk," were worn in town (a beanie makes a good modern alternative), and wide-brimmed, low-crowned ones were worn when riding or traveling. "Sugar-sack" hats came in various shapes: one was something like an Egyptian fez with a more rounded top; another resembles the one worn in the Arnolfini marriage portrait. These hats can be made from an oblong of felt sewn into a cylinder, with a round "lid" sewn on and the bottom edge rolled into a brim.

Right: It's difficult to say which is
more ridiculous—the men's
elongated shoes or the ladies'
headdresses. Note also that the
lady in the middle is wearing a fur
cutaway overtunic.

Up to about 1430, women's hats were remarkable for their width. The
simplest was the chaplet, or "cushion" hat—a thick, padded ring that held
down a filigree net containing the coils of hair above each ear. Another
style used "templers" (or templettes) positioned on either side
of the forehead to enclose the hair and support a veil. These templers
grew wider and more exaggerated until they reached beyond the
shoulders. The most elaborate styles used wire structures to produce
shapes such as cows' horns or butterfly wings, which were usually draped
with a veil. Some of these styles can still be seen in the headdresses of
French or Italian regional costume and also in those of some orders of
nuns, especially in France.

In the mid-1400s, width gave way to height. The padded roll was now
bent upward to form a deep V shape, decorated with jewels and a veil.
What most people think of as the typical medieval headdress is the
hennin, a tall pointed hat with a veil attached. This is easy to make by
covering a cone of cardboard or wire mesh with a light, gauzy fabric—but
wearing the hennin takes practice.

BELTS AND GIRDLES

Girdles were worn by both sexes with the slim-fitting cotehardie. They were made from leather (men only) and silk braid or any thick silken cord, often with several strands braided together. Girdles could be of any length and were slung low on the hips and knotted in front, the joining point often covered with a brooch or metal fastening. Illustrations of a later period, however, show what look more like ordinary belts, at the natural waist or slightly above. Men can get away with a plain leather belt as long as it's soft, has an old-fashioned tongued buckle that isn't shiny (distressing always helps), and doesn't have a loop to keep the long end neat.

Hanging from the girdle would be a number of accessories, including a pouch. You can make a simple pouch from a circle of fabric by punching holes around the edge and threading a drawstring through them. Purses for nobles were far more elaborate: flat, fastened with a flap, and usually embroidered, often with metal thread. Men's purses were threaded onto the belt through two holes.

BOOKS

Books were precious since they were produced, written, and illustrated entirely by hand. A "girdle book" was enclosed in a binding of cloth or animal skin that had a long tail with a knot in the end, which was tucked into the girdle. The book, fastened shut with clasps, hung upside down so that it could be picked up and read easily. However, since only a small proportion of the population could read and write, you must ensure that you give a book only to a suitable character.

STOCKINGS AND GARTERS

Stockings, or hose, were always made of wool or linen: knitting would not be well known in Europe until the 1400s. Stockings were cut on the bias to fit as closely as possible and sewn up the back. Women wore thigh-

Left: An unusually detailed little wooden figure from 1470 clearly shows the man's purse hanging from his belt.

STYLE TIP

Don't have pockets in any garments—they didn't appear until the Elizabethan period. Medieval folk carried everything they needed slung from the girdle or belt. Fitchets, or pocketlike slits in the side seam of garments, only appear around 1250, and even then they were only a means of accessing objects slung from a girdle inside the main garment, not actual sewn pockets.

length hose, held up by a garter just above the knee, although owing to the length of the gown, they were hardly ever seen. Men's hose could be rolled down to just below the knee for active work and tied or secured by a garter. Today's stretchy materials work well for hose: sweatshirt fabric, fluffy side out, gives a good, close fit.

SHOES

Shoes came in shapes from square toes to pointy to extremely pointy and back to sensible roundness. However, they were always flat, without any heel. Cutout patterns on the front were popular: in his "Miller's Tale," Chaucer mentions a character with "[Saint] Paul's windows carven on his shoes." Long pointy shoes were, of course, only for the fashionable and idle: the shape of ordinary footwear simply followed that of the foot into a gentle point. If you're making shoes from scratch, see online agencies for a simple pattern. However, some modern shoes and boots can be worn, as long as they are flat-soled and don't have modern fastenings (eyelets and laces, zippers, and Velcro are out). Flat leather sandals in plain brown can be customized for working-class characters, while some modern fashion boots in distressed leather, with side buckles, are a happy revival.

GLOVES

Gloves were virtually unknown until the twelfth century and still rare by the end of the thirteenth, although women of high status wore linen gloves to protect their fair hands from sunburn. By 1349, however, everybody owned a pair and the Guild of Glovers was established as a separate organization. Remember, though, that the nobility

Left: This stained-glass window image shows a wide-brimmed traveling hat worn with a hood or possibly a wimple underneath. Because these hats were worn by both sexes, it's hard to tell if this is a man or a woman.

Left: Although the pin is missing, this is a fine example of a thirteenth-century ring brooch. It was found in Coventry, England, in 1937. Solid, heavy, and studded with as many jewels as possible, it's typical of the jewelry of the period.

carried theirs—gauntlet style, with cuffs of embroidered silk—in the hand rather than wore them. Working gloves were of coarse, thick material, with three divisions: for thumb, forefinger, and the other three.

JEWELRY

Jewelry was substantial and showy. Necklaces, for both sexes, were heavy and studded with jewels, as were coronets. Brooches came in many forms. A cluster brooch was a large gemstone surrounded by clusters of small pearls. Of more practical use, a ring brooch was a circular fastening with a hinged pin. Bracelets, rings, and pendants were also worn. Many of these can be replicated using resins, plastic foam, or fiberglass, and there are many Web sites specializing in replica jewelry. Cameos were newly popular, as were fede-ring brooches, featuring two hands clasped in betrothal.

The early 1400s saw a vogue for "folly bells," small bells hung from the belt or sewn to clothing that produced a tinkling sound when the wearer moved or danced. Tiny brass or silver bells like these can be found in many craft stores.

PASSERSBY

"*Sometimes a troop of damsels glad,*
An abbot on an ambling pad,
Sometimes a curly shepherd lad,
Or long-hair'd page in crimson clad,
Goes by to tower'd Camelot:
And sometimes thro' the mirror blue
The knights come riding two and two:
She hath no loyal knight and true,
The Lady of Shalott."

Alfred Tennyson, *The Lady of Shallot*, 1842

FROM LORD TO SERF

Gatherings such as tournaments, jousting, and fairs brought together crowds of people of all classes. Finely dressed lords and ladies watched the jousting from the stands, while the common folk milled around enjoying the entertainment provided by jugglers, jesters, ballad singers, and acrobats. This chapter looks at the various medieval characters you might meet there and want to re-create.

THE TOURNAMENT

Knights were the sporting celebrities of their day. They traveled from miles around to take part in a tournament, pitching their gaily colored tents nearby and parading in full armor on the opening day. Each would have carried his own heraldic banner, identifying him to the crowd.

Below: Present-day tournaments are very popular, although in our safety-conscious age, riders perform solo feats rather than charging at each other.

Jousting involved two knights riding at each other in full armor, helmeted and with lances drawn, each attempting to knock the other from his horse. The horses were also fully armed and decorated, with a surcoat over the body and armor over the head. Even then it was a great opportunity for dressing up and role-playing. Knights who might never have been on Crusade re-enacted ancient battles with "opponents" dressed as Saracens.

RELIGIOUS FOLK

The clergy made up a large and visible section of medieval society. While monks and nuns were confined within their houses, there would certainly have been a number of wandering friars in the crowd. Not attached to any particular church, they lived among the people and survived by begging. A friar would be wearing a long robe of some rough material (black for Dominicans, brown for Franciscans), belted with a knotted rope, and

CROWDS IN SCARLET

Dressing in red often indicated dignity and importance. In 1486, Henry VII visited the town of York. Eager to make a good impression, the mayor sent out a decree stating what each person on the welcoming committee should wear. He and the senior members of the council would be wearing long scarlet gowns, while the more junior council members and the city clerk would be in violet and chamberlains (managers of the great households) in murrey (purple-red). Any other citizens attending also had to wear red. This horseback procession, which rode out to meet the king five miles from the town, must have made an impact.

Left: In the *Brother Cadfael* TV series, Derek Jacobi (left) plays a Benedictine monk at Shrewsbury Abbey in the English county of Shropshire. The stories are set in about 1140.

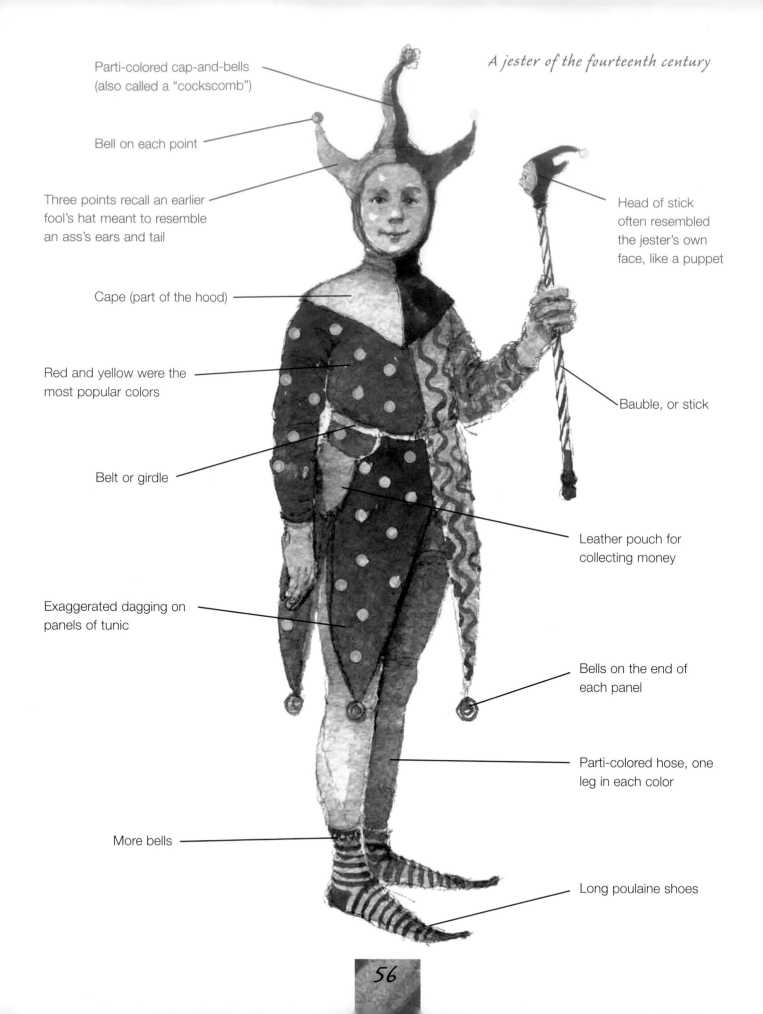

A jester of the fourteenth century

Parti-colored cap-and-bells (also called a "cockscomb")

Bell on each point

Three points recall an earlier fool's hat meant to resemble an ass's ears and tail

Cape (part of the hood)

Red and yellow were the most popular colors

Belt or girdle

Exaggerated dagging on panels of tunic

More bells

Head of stick often resembled the jester's own face, like a puppet

Bauble, or stick

Leather pouch for collecting money

Bells on the end of each panel

Parti-colored hose, one leg in each color

Long poulaine shoes

leather sandals. He would probably carry a staff and a wooden bowl for offerings. Men will be relieved to know that tonsure wigs can be found on costume Web sites.

COOKS

A cook would wear the usual working person's dress, with a long apron tied around the neck. He might be selling roast ox or pig (not on a hot dog bun!) or sweets such as gingerbread, from a tray hung around his neck.

ENTERTAINERS

Acrobats, jesters, and jugglers were likely to be wearing parti-colored costume—perhaps a thigh-length tunic, half in red and half in yellow, along with hose of the same alternating colors. This gave a dazzling quartered effect, guaranteed to attract a crowd. A long and elaborately dagged liripipe on the hood might be decorated with folly bells.

PILGRIMS

There would certainly be pilgrims, wearing homespun russet tunics belted with cord and rough travel-stained cloaks. They also wore a low, broad-brimmed hat decorated with the badges of the shrines they had visited. This was a matter of some pride: only those who had been to Santiago de Compostella in Spain were allowed to wear the distinctive shell badge, but there were many others, including that of St. Thomas Becket in Canterbury, England. The medal of St. Christopher, patron saint of travelers, was also popular. Either round or in the shape of a

LADIES' FINERY

"These tournaments are attended by many ladies of the first rank and greatest beauty . . . They are dressed in parti-coloured tunics, one half being of one colour and the other half of another, with short hoods and liripipes which are wrapped about their heads like cords; their girdles are handsomely ornamented with gold and silver, and they wear short swords and daggers before them in pouches, a little below the navel; and thus habited they are mounted on the finest horses that can be procured and ornamented with the richest furniture. "

Henry Knighton, *Chronicle*, c.1360

STYLE TIP

The most authentic way to wear a belt is to choose one a lot longer than your usual waist size. You may need to make more holes so that it fits. Make sure it has an old-fashioned buckle with a tongue. Place the belt around your tunic at waist level, buckle it loosely, then take the long end over and behind the buckle so that it hangs down.

cross, it showed the saint carrying the Christ child on his shoulders. Pilgrims also carried a wooden staff and a leather water bottle.

CHILDREN

Older children wore miniature versions of their parents' clothes, but toddlers, regardless of sex, were dressed alike in long wool gowns. Girls up to the age of sixteen were allowed to have their long hair unbound but might wear a simple veil or circlet for the tournament outing. Babies were swaddled, or bound in layers of linen, and their heads were wrapped in a linen coif. Historians believe they were often carried strapped to a backboard, a forerunner of today's backpack-style carrier.

WEDDING AND MOURNING

There might also be a bride and groom, celebrating their marriage. Although black had come to be the color of mourning by the mid-fourteenth century, no particular color was associated with marriage. The bride and groom simply wore a particularly elaborate version of their everyday clothes, and the bride had a circlet of flowers. However, green was a popular color for the dress since it symbolized the hoped-for fertility. Modern "medieval" weddings feature favors such as silver

Right: The guests at this medieval-themed wedding in Bavaria have managed to avoid most of the medieval costume pitfalls. This image shows the traditional headdresses worn by brides and their attendants.

charms, foil-covered chocolate coins, and herb sachets. None of these is authentic! Widows were expected to wear dark and modest gowns and wimples or veils long after they had gone out of fashion elsewhere.

LOW LIFE—AND ROBIN HOOD

There were also pickpockets, moneylenders, fortune-tellers, ladies of easy virtue, and the odd outlaw. It was easy to find yourself beyond the law in medieval Europe, where the lower classes were still little more than peasants and laws were severe. The most famous outlaw was Robin Hood, the Earl of Loxley, unjustly deprived of his lands on returning from the Crusades and condemned to a life on the run in Sherwood Forest. He is usually shown dressed in a short green tunic and hose, often decorated with dagging, and a pointed cap.

OTHER TRADES

The tournament circuit, and knighthood generally, supported many associated trades, keeping armorers, boot makers, leatherworkers, and tailors busy, as well as farriers and grooms. They would all be mingling with the crowd at the tournament, wearing some variant of workingman's clothing and almost certainly an apron.

Left: Errol Flynn defined most people's idea of Robin Hood in 1938. The dagged leather jerkin is quite convincing, but the tights and lace-up boots were dreamed up by the wardrobe department.

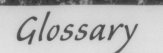

Glossary

barbet A band placed under the chin and fastened on the top of the head, worn by women in the twelfth through fourteenth centuries.

bias cut Cutting cloth so that the weave hangs diagonally rather than across and up/down. This gives a more flexible hang.

brocade Any rich, stiff silk fabric with a pattern woven into it.

canvas A coarse cloth made of hemp or linen.

caparison A decorated covering for a horse.

circlet A narrow metal headband worn by ranks below the nobility.

city-state A region controlled by a ruling city, especially in medieval Italy.

cloth of gold Fabric including silk threads wrapped in gold.

coat of arms The badge of a great family.

coif A close-fitting cap of white linen tied under the chin, worn by both sexes and by infants.

coronet A circlet for the head.

Crusades Wars conducted by European Christians, largely against Muslims, to control the Holy Land.

dagging Where hems and ends of bands are cut in various patterns.

damask A reversible, patterned fabric made of linen, silk, or wool.

doublet A short, quilted, or padded jerkin with a front opening, worn by men from the fourteenth century on.

feudal Owing allegiance to a lord.

filigree Delicate ornamental work of twisted gold, silver, or other wire.

fillet A woven or metal band worn around the head.

flax A blue-flowered plant whose fibrous stems are made into cloth.

fustian A coarse cloth made of brushed cotton weft and linen warp.

gorget A linen neck-covering.

hauberk A long coat of chain mail, often sleeveless.

hose Leg coverings made of wool or linen.

jupon A doublet made of padded, quilted material.

liripipe The long, exaggerated tail-like end of a hood, which hung like a streamer.

litter A seat or bed slung between two poles and carried by men.

livery Uniform worn by servants.

mail or chain mail Armor made of interlocking rows of metal rings.

mantle Loose, sleeveless cloak.

muslin A very fine, gauzy cotton fabric.

parti-color(ed) Divided vertically in half, in two colors of cloth.

pattens Raised wooden soles attached to shoes to keep them out of the mud.

points Ties for attaching hose to braies.

poulaines Long, pointed shoes.

revers Parts of a garment, especially lapels, turned back to show the reverse side.

russet A reddish brown color; also a coarse cloth of that color.

serge A hard-wearing wool fabric.

Silk Road An ancient trade route connecting Asia with Europe.

snood A kind of hairnet, often of fine gold wire.

surcoat An overcoat or, in military wear, the tunic worn over armor.

tabard A sleeveless outer garment with open side seams.

tippet A liripipe; a cape; or a streamer from the elbow of the cotehardie.

train The extended hem of a dress that trails behind on the ground.

velvet A soft, thick-piled fabric made of silk.

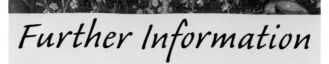

Further Information

BOOKS

GENERAL

Diehl, Daniel, and Mark Donnelly. *Medieval Celebrations: How to Plan for Holidays, Weddings, and Re-enactments with Recipes, Customs, Costumes, Decorations, Songs, Dances, and Games.* Stackpole Books, 2001.

Elliott, Lynne. *Clothing in the Middle Ages.* Crabtree, 2004.

Hartley, Dorothy. *Medieval Costume and How to Recreate It.* Dover, 2003.

Houston, Mary G. *Medieval Costume in England and France: The 13th, 14th and 15th Centuries.* Dover, 1996.

Hunniset, Jean. *Period Costume for Stage & Screen: Patterns for Women's Dress, Medieval–1500.* Players Press, 1996.

Norris, Herbert. *Medieval Costume and Fashion.* Dover, 1998.

Piponnier, Françoise, and Perrine Mane. *Dress in the Middle Ages.* Yale University Press, 2000.

Thursfield, Sarah. *Medieval Tailor's Assistant: Making Common Garments 1200–1500.* Costume & Fashion Press, 2001.

YOUNGER READERS

Langley, Andrew. *Medieval Life.* Eyewitness Books, 1996.

Steele, Philip. *History of Costume and Fashion: The Medieval World.* Facts On File, 2005.

Tierney, Tom. *Medieval Costumes, Paper Dolls.* Dover, 1996.

WEB SITES

Many of these Web sites have links to other, related sites.

www.bnf.fr/enluminures/accueil.htm
One thousand illustrations from illuminated manuscripts, including Books of Hours, calendars, and much more, relating to King Charles V (1338–80).

www.costumes.org
The Costumer's Manifesto—information and patterns.

www.fordham.edu/halsall/medfilms.html
Listing of movies with a medieval setting.

www.mnsu.edu/emuseum/history/middleages/
Good general introduction to the period and links to other sites.

www.sapphireandsage.com/bodice.html
Reproduction jewelry: primarily a selling site but has good images.

www.sca.org
The Society for Creative Anachronism, an international organization that explores the culture of pre-seventeenth-century Europe. The costume page has instructions on making clothing.

www.sewingcentral.com
Patterns for sale, plus advice on making costumes.

www.virtue.to/articles/
Instructions on making costumes and on modern fabrics.

RE-ENACTMENT EVENTS

There are medieval re-enactment events all over the United States. Several of the Web sites above also have event listings.

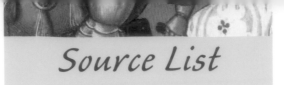

Source List

A selection of plays, movies, TV series, and musicals with medieval themes.

PLAYS

Becket (1959), by Jean Anouilh

The Boy With a Cart (1939); *The Lady's Not for Burning* (1948); *The Lark* (1955); *Curtmantle* (1961)—all by Christopher Fry

Edward III; *Richard II*; *Henry IV, Part 1*; *Henry IV, Part 2*; *Henry V*; *Henry VI, Part 1*; *Henry VI, Part 2*; *Henry VI, Part 3*; *Richard III*—all by William Shakespeare

Medieval Mystery Play Cycles: York, Wakefield, Towneley, Chester (UK)

Murder in the Cathedral (1935), by T. S. Eliot

The Mysteries (1985), by Tony Harrison

STAGE MUSICALS

The Lord of the Rings (2007)

Spamalot (2005)

MOVIES AND TV

KING ARTHUR

Camelot (1967), dir. Joshua Logan, with Richard Harris, Vanessa Redgrave

A Connecticut Yankee (1931), dir. David Butler, with Will Rogers, Maureen O'Sullivan

A Connecticut Yankee in King Arthur's Court (1949), dir. Tay Garnett, with Bing Crosby, Rhonda Fleming

Excalibur (1981), dir. John Boorman, with Nigel Terry, Helen Mirren

First Knight (1995), dir. Jerry Zucker, with Sean Connery, Richard Gere

A Knight in Camelot (1998), dir. Roger Young, with Whoopi Goldberg, Michael York

Knights of the Round Table (1953), dir. Richard Thorpe, with Robert Taylor, Ava Gardner

A Knight's Tale (2001), dir. Brian Helgeland, with Heath Ledger, Rufus Sewell

Lancelot du Lac (1974), dir. Robert Bresson, with Luc Simon, Laura Duke Condominas

The Mists of Avalon (2001), dir. Udi Edel, with Anjelica Huston, Julianna Marguiles (TV movie)

Monty Python and the Holy Grail (1975), dir. Terry Gilliam, Terry Jones, with Graham Chapman

KNIGHTS AND CRUSADES

Black Arrow (1985), dir. John Hough, with Oliver Reed, Fernando Rey (TV movie)

The Black Shield of Falworth (1954), dir. Rudolph Maté, with Tony Curtis, Janet Leigh

The Crusades (1935), dir. Cecil B. de Mille, with Henry Wilcoxon, Loretta Young

Gawain and the Green Knight (1973), dir. Stephen Weeks, with Murray Head, Nigel Green

Ivanhoe (1952), dir. Richard Thorpe, with Robert Taylor, Elizabeth Taylor

Ivanhoe (1958–9), dir. various, with Roger Moore (TV series)

Ivanhoe (1982), dir. Douglas Camfield, with Anthony Andrews, James Mason (TV movie)

Ivanhoe (1997), dir. Stuart Orme, with Steven Waddington, Christopher Lee (TV miniseries)

King Richard and the Crusaders (1954), dir. David Butler, with Rex Harrison, George Sanders

Sword of the Valiant: The Legend of Sir Gawain and the Green Knight (1984), dir. Stephen Weeks, with Sean Connery, Miles O'Keeffe

ROBIN HOOD

The Adventures of Robin Hood (1938), dir. William Keighley, Michael Curtiz, with Errol Flynn

The Adventures of Robin Hood (1955–60), dir. various, with Richard Greene (TV series)

The Bandit of Sherwood Forest (1946), dir. George Sherman, Henry Levin, with Cornel Wilde

Men of Sherwood Forest (1954), dir. Val Guest, with Don Taylor, Reginald Beckwith

Prince of Thieves (1948), dir. Howard Bretherton, with Jon Hall, Patricia Morison

Robin Hood (1922), dir. Allan Dwan, with Douglas Fairbanks, Wallace Beery

Robin Hood (1991), dir. John Irvin, with Patrick Bergin, Uma Thurman

Robin Hood (2006), dir. various, with Jonas Armstrong, Keith Allen (TV series)

Robin Hood: Men in Tights (1993), dir Mel Brooks, with Cary Elwes, Richard Lewis

Robin Hood: Prince of Thieves (1991), dir. Kevin Reynolds, with Kevin Costner, Morgan Freeman

Robin and Marian (1976), dir. Richard Lester, with Sean Connery, Audrey Hepburn

Rogues of Sherwood Forest (1950), dir. Gordon Douglas, with John Derek, George MacCready

The Story of Robin Hood and His Merrie Men (1952), dir. Ken Annakin, with Richard Todd

Sword of Sherwood Forest (1960), dir. Terence Fisher, with Richard Greene, Peter Cushing

OTHER HISTORICAL MOVIES

Alexander Nevsky (1938), dir. Sergei Eisenstein, with Nikolai Cherkassov, Nikolai Okhlopkov

Becket (1964), dir. Peter Glenville, with Richard Burton, Peter O'Toole

Braveheart (1995), dir. Mel Gibson, with Mel Gibson, Sophie Marceau

The Bruce (1996), dir. Bob Carruthers, David McWhinnie, with Oliver Reed, Brian Blessed

Cadfael (1994), dir. Sebastian Graham Jones, with Derek Jacobi (TV series)

The Canterbury Tales (1971), dir. Pier Paolo Pasolini, with Pier Paolo Pasolini, Hugh Griffith

El Cid (1961) dir. Anthony Mann, with Charlton Heston, Sophia Loren

Henry V (1945), dir. Laurence Olivier, with Laurence Oliver, George Robey

Henry V (1989), dir. Kenneth Branagh, with Kenneth Branagh, Derek Jacobi

Joan of Arc (1948), dir. Victor Fleming, with Ingrid Bergman, José Ferrer

The Lion in Winter (1968), dir. Anthony Harvey, with Katherine Hepburn, Peter O'Toole

Man of La Mancha (1972), dir. Arthur Hiller, with Peter O'Toole, Sophia Loren

The Name of the Rose (1986), dir. Jean-Jacques Annaud, with Sean Connery, F. Murray Abraham

Richard III (1955), dir. Laurence Olivier, with Laurence Olivier, Claire Bloom

Saint Joan (1957), dir. Otto Preminger, with Jean Seberg, Richard Widmark

The Seventh Seal (1957), dir. Ingmar Bergman, with Max von Sydow, Bengt Ekerot

Throne of Blood (1957), dir. Akira Kurosawa, with Hideo Oguni, Shinobu Hashimoto

Tower of London (1939), dir. Rowland V. Lee, with Basil Rathbone, Boris Karloff

MEDIEVAL FANTASY

The Lord of the Rings movie trilogy: *The Fellowship of the Ring* (2001), *The Two Towers* (2002), and *The Return of the King* (2003), dir. Peter Jackson, with Ian McKellen, Cate Blanchett

The Chronicles of Narnia: The Lion, the Witch, and the Wardrobe (2005), *Prince Caspian* (2008), dir. Andrew Adamson, with Tilda Swinton, James McAvoy

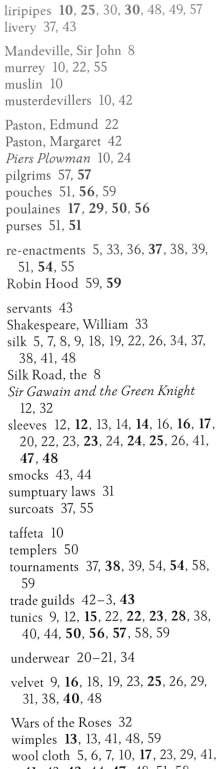

Numbers in **bold** refer to illustrations.